SAMUEL D. HUNTER

Samuel D. Hunter grew up i
York City. His full-length pl
Desk Award, Lucille Lortel ....g Play,
GLAAD Media Award, Drama League and Outer Critics
Circle nominations for Best Play), *A Case for the Existence
of God* (New York Drama Critics' Circle Award for Best
Play, Hull-Warriner Award), *Little Bear Ridge Road* (Jeff
Award, Best New Work), *Grangeville* (Drama Desk and
Outer Critics Circle nomination for Best Play), *A Bright
New Boise* (Obie Award, Drama Desk nomination for Best
Play), *Greater Clements* (Drama Desk nomination for Best
Play, Outer Critics Circle Honoree), *Lewiston/Clarkston*
(Drama Desk nomination for Best Play), *The Few, A Great
Wilderness, Rest, Pocatello, The Healing* and *The Harvest*,
among others.

The film version of *The Whale*, directed by Darren Aronofsky
and starring Brendan Fraser, was nominated for the 2023
BAFTA Award for Best Adapted Screenplay and received two
Oscars, including Best Actor. He was also a writer and producer
on all four seasons of FX's *Baskets*. He is the recipient of a
2014 MacArthur 'Genius Grant' Fellowship, a 2012 Whiting
Writers Award and an honorary doctorate from the University of
Idaho.

His work has been produced Off Broadway in New York City
by Lincoln Center Theatre, Playwrights Horizons, LCT3,
Signature Theatre, Page 73 Productions, Clubbed Thumb, and
Rattlestick Playwrights Theatre. Elsewhere, his work has been
produced by Theatre Royal Bath, Theatre Rotterdam, Dallas
Theatre Center, Seattle Rep, Denver Center for the Performing
Arts, Woolly Mammoth Theatre Company, South Coast Rep
and Victory Gardens, among others. Two published anthologies
of his work are available from TCG Books, and another is
forthcoming. He is a member of the Dramatists Guild Council
and a current Resident Playwright at the Signature Theatre
in New York City. He holds degrees in playwriting from
NYU, The Iowa Playwrights Workshop, and Juilliard.

Samuel D. Hunter

CLARKSTON

NICK HERN BOOKS

London

www.nickhernbooks.co.uk

A Nick Hern Book

Clarkston first published in Great Britain as a paperback original in 2025 by Nick Hern Books Limited, The Glasshouse, 49a Goldhawk Road, London W12 8QP

Clarkston copyright © 2025 Samuel D. Hunter

Samuel D. Hunter has asserted his right to be identified as the author of this work

Cover design by FEAST; photography by Emilio Madrid

Designed and typeset by Nick Hern Books, London
Printed in Great Britain by Mimeo Ltd, Huntingdon, Cambridgeshire PE29 6XX

A CIP catalogue record for this book is available from the British Library

ISBN 978 1 83904 513 4

www.nickhernbooks.co.uk/environmental-policy

Nick Hern Books' authorised representative in the EU is
Easy Access System Europe – Mustamäe tee 50, 10621 Tallinn, Estonia
email gpsr.requests@easproject.com

Clarkston was first performed at Dallas Theater Center, Texas (Kevin Moriarty, Artistic Director), on 3 December 2015. The cast was as follows:

JAKE	Taylor Trensch
CHRIS	Sam Lilja
TRISHA	Heidi Armbruster

Director	Davis McCallum
Set Designer	Andrew Boyce
Costume Designer	Jessica Pabst
Lighting Designer	Eric Southern
Sound Designer	Stowe Nelson
Dramaturg	John M. Baker
Stage Manager	Kirstin Jones

It was performed as part of a double bill with *Lewiston* by Samuel D. Hunter at the Rattlestick Playwrights Theater, New York City (Daniella Topol, Artistic Director), on 10 October 2018. The cast was as follows:

JAKE	Noah Robbins
CHRIS	Edmund Donovan
TRISHA	Heidi Armbruster

Director	Davis McCallum
Set Designer	Dane Laffrey
Costume Designer	Jessica Wegener Shay
Lighting Designer	Stacey Derosier
Sound Designer	Fitz Patton
Dramaturg	John M. Baker
Stage Managers	Katie Young
	Joanne Pan

Clarkston received its British premiere at Trafalgar Theatre, London, on 25 September 2025 (previews from 17 September), produced by OHenry Productions and LD Entertainment. The cast was as follows:

JAKE	Joe Locke
CHRIS	Ruaridh Mollica
TRISHA	Sophie Melville

Understudies

JAKE & CHRIS	Kai Davies
TRISHA	Lizzie Clarke

Director	Jack Serio
Set and Costume Designer	Milla Clarke
Lighting Designer	Stacey Derosier
Sound Designer	George Dennis
Dramaturg	John M. Baker
Voice and Dialect Coach	Hazel Holder
Associate Director	Natalie Simone
Associate Lighting Designer	Tom Turner
Casting Director	Stuart Burt CDG
Casting Consultant	Taylor Williams

Characters

JAKE, *early to mid-twenties, male*
CHRIS, *early to mid-twenties, male*
TRISHA, *late thirties to early forties, female*

Setting

Various locations in and around a Costco in Clarkston, Washington. The store is on the edge of town, at the bank of the Snake River at the Idaho border.

The space should have the overall feeling of a parking lot. The different sections of the store should be created very simply, perhaps just with large metal shelves that rotate and move to denote the change in location. Every scene (except for the final scene) should have an oppressive, industrial feel.

Notes

Dialogue written in *italics* is emphatic, deliberate; dialogue in ALL CAPS is impulsive, explosive.

A forward slash (/) indicates an overlap in dialogue. Whenever the slash appears, the following line of dialogue should begin.

Ellipses (…) indicate when a character is trailing off, dashes (–) indicate where a character is being cut off, either by another character or themselves.

Dialogue in [brackets] is implied, not spoken.

No intermission.

This text went to press before the end of rehearsals and so may differ slightly from the play as performed.

Scene One

Food Department: Snacks.

Massive metal shelves stocked intermittently with different brands of potato chips, all in gigantic bags, along with other items: licorice, candycorn, gummy bears, etc.

CHRIS *enters, pulling a palette on wheels with two large boxes full of items to be stocked. He is tall and broad, but not movie-star attractive by any means. He is followed by* JAKE, *nearly the physical opposite of* CHRIS: *small, thin, nearly delicate.*

They both wear Costco uniforms.

CHRIS. Just tell Janet you don't want to work full shifts with him. If you get stuck with him for a few hours then you'll be fine, but if you get stuck with a / full shift –

JAKE. Wait he's not like dangerous though, is he?

CHRIS. Oh no, no. Well maybe.

JAKE. I mean was he in prison for something / really [bad] – ?

CHRIS. It was just a drug thing, I think, I mean I'm sure he [isn't violent] –

Pause.

Sorry, I'm not trying to scare you.

CHRIS *starts taking the packing materials off one of the boxes, opening them up.*

JAKE. No, I'm not, I'm –

Pause.

I'm just glad you're the one training me.

CHRIS. Yeah they don't let him train people anymore. Few years ago he was training this Nez Perce kid and he was being like *super* racist.

JAKE. Oh wow does he still work here?!

CHRIS. What?

JAKE. The – The Indian – Native American kid.

CHRIS. No. Why?

JAKE. Oh it's just – That's cool. That he was a Native – first peoples.

CHRIS *looks at him quizzically.* JAKE *smiles back awkwardly.*

CHRIS. Where are you from again?

JAKE. Connecticut.

CHRIS. Okay.

JAKE. Town on the coast called Waterford.

CHRIS. You don't have Indians there?

JAKE. I mean, where I'm from is the unceded land of the Pequot and Mohegan peoples? But they aren't many around anymore, it's really fucked up. I made my dad put a land acknowledgement on the front door of our house.

Awkward pause. CHRIS *looks at him.*

Huh.

CHRIS....Cool.

Pause.

CHRIS *starts stocking the shelves.* JAKE *watches him for a moment, not doing anything.* CHRIS *stocks a few items, then looks at* JAKE.

What?

JAKE. Oh, I'm just – I mean I'm ready for the training.

Pause.

CHRIS. Okay.

JAKE. So what do I do?

CHRIS. You take the stuff and put it on the shelf.

Pause.

That's basically the training.

JAKE. Oh. Cool.

JAKE reaches into the box, takes out some items and starts throwing them on the shelf haphazardly.

CHRIS stocks a few more items, looking at him.

CHRIS. I mean you have to like put them in rows.

JAKE. So there's more training.

CHRIS demonstrates shelving items.

CHRIS. Here, just – Like this. If there's any products on the shelf already, bring that forward and stack the new products in the back. And just be sure that you face the items in the front.

JAKE. Oh awesome.

CHRIS. Yeah it's really not.

They both continue to stock items. Silence as they work. In the background, the somewhat loud whir of a forklift.

You're a long way from / home.

JAKE. What?

CHRIS. I said *you're a long way from home.*

JAKE. Oh. Yeah.

CHRIS. You out here for school?

JAKE. Oh no, I graduated couple years ago.

CHRIS. You got family out here?

JAKE (*oddly excited*). Well no but I have a family connection to the area!

Pause.

CHRIS. Okay?

The forklift sound suddenly cuts off.

JAKE (*still loud*). I'm related to – !

(*Short pause, quieter.*) Actually I'm a descendant of William Clark.

Pause.

CHRIS. Oh.

JAKE (*smiling*). Yeah.

CHRIS. Like the – ?

JAKE. Yeah like Lewis and Clark, the explorers. I'm related to him.

CHRIS. Huh, that's [interesting] –

Pause.

Sorry, what's your name again?

JAKE. Jake.

CHRIS. Jake.

Pause.

Huh. Jake Clark, that's cool.

JAKE. Oh, no, it's – Actually Clark isn't my last name.

CHRIS. Oh.

JAKE. I'm not like – I mean I'm not like a *super direct* descendant. But my dad's cousin is a Clark.

CHRIS. So what's your last name?

JAKE. Baumgartner-Pepperdine.

Pause.

My parents are assholes.

They continue to stock.

JAKE. You grow up in Clarkston?

CHRIS. Lewiston. Across the river.

JAKE. In Idaho!

CHRIS. Yep.

JAKE. That's really neat.

Pause.

CHRIS. Okay.

Silence. They continue to work.

So why'd you come out here?

Pause. JAKE *stops working for a moment, thinking.* CHRIS *looks at him.*

You okay?

JAKE. Yeah, sorry, I – I mean it's something I've always wanted to do. Go out west, follow the Lewis and Clark trail. And I've never even seen the Pacific, it's ridiculous.

CHRIS. Huh. I've never seen it either.

Pause.

JAKE. Wait *really*?

CHRIS. Nope.

JAKE. You live like three hundred miles from the ocean and you've never seen it?

CHRIS. Just never had the chance, I guess.

JAKE. Wait so have you ever seen an ocean at all?

CHRIS. No. I mean like, photographs obviously, but – No.

JAKE. Not even like a family trip?

CHRIS. My family isn't –

Pause.

I just haven't traveled a lot. Didn't even leave town for college.

JAKE. You went to –?

CHRIS. LCSC, in Lewiston. English major. It was okay. I had like two good professors. Two and a half. Where'd you go?

JAKE. Bennington? It's like a little liberal arts school in Vermont.

CHRIS. What'd you major in?

JAKE. Post-Colonial Gender Studies.

Pause.

CHRIS. Huh.

Pause.

That's like – a thing you can study?

JAKE. The way the school works is you make up your own major.

CHRIS. Oh.

JAKE. It's actually pretty cool, the student is like really empowered there. At the end of each course the students grade the teacher.

CHRIS. And that – works?

JAKE. Yeah it's great. I mean who's to say that the professor knows more than their students?

CHRIS. Isn't it like – their *job* to know more than their students?

Pause.

JAKE *doesn't know how to respond. They continue to work.*

Emily's also one you don't want to get stuck with on the overnight. I mean she's fine and everything, she's totally nice, but she's just – She has all these weird pictures of her iguana, it's like – Anyway she's nice.

Pause.

Here, why don't you open that box?

CHRIS *hands him his box cutter.*

JAKE. Oh sure.

JAKE has a small involuntary movement in his hand, he drops the box cutter on the floor. CHRIS watches him.

CHRIS. You [okay]…?

JAKE. Yeah, sorry.

JAKE grabs the box cutter, then cuts the plastic tape off the box. He reaches over the box, struggling to open it. Finally he gets the lid open.

CHRIS stops.

CHRIS. You know, you –

Pause.

You have to be able to lift sixty pounds?

JAKE looks at CHRIS.

Pause.

I mean, the – I'm not trying to be a dick but that's one of the requirements for the overnight stocker job, you have to be able to lift sixty pounds. If you can't then it just makes it really hard for whoever you're working with, they end up having to take up the / slack –

JAKE. I can lift sixty pounds. I can lift *more* than sixty / pounds.

CHRIS. Oh, cool, I was just [making sure] –

JAKE. I just accidentally dropped / the –

CHRIS. Okay, sorry. Sorry.

Pause.

JAKE goes back to his work, quietly annoyed. He reaches into the box, pulling out large, heavy plastic tubs of popcorn kernels. Silence as they continue to stock.

CHRIS feels badly, tries to re-engage him.

We learned quite a bit about Lewis and Clark in elementary school. There was this guy who does like – impersonations of both Lewis and Clark? That's not the right word, he's not like an *actor*, he's a historian I think, I remember him being like, 'President Jefferson sent me and my friend William Clark to explore the – '

JAKE *loses his grip on the tub, it falls to the floor, spilling everywhere.* CHRIS *sees him.*

JAKE. *Fuck.*

CHRIS. Okay, why are you doing / that?

JAKE. I'm not – I'm sorry, I just dropped it –

CHRIS. Again, I'm not trying to be a dick, but you can't do this job if you / can't even carry these –

JAKE. I'm fine, really –

CHRIS. There's other jobs here, the night shift sucks anyway –

JAKE. There's nothing else, I checked –

CHRIS. Look, lemme just grab Janet and we can / see if –

JAKE. I have Huntington's disease.

CHRIS *stops.*

Pause.

CHRIS. What?

JAKE. It's a degenerative neurological disease, and I have this variant of it called juvenile Huntington's, which means it sort of progresses quicker / than –

CHRIS. I mean I don't really know / what [this means] –

JAKE. So sometimes I might have to take a break or – there's a thing called chorea where sometimes I have involuntary movements which is what that was, but *really* it's not that bad normally, I just need to be careful with – Look it's not a big deal.

Pause.

CHRIS. Did you tell Janet when she hired you?

JAKE. No.

CHRIS. So why did you tell me?

JAKE. Because if we're working together and you think I'm doing something weird or moving strangely, if I need to take a little break or something, / just –

CHRIS. But I mean you – You think this is the best job for you?

JAKE. Look the pay is like twice what I'd be making at a McDonald's and probably even more than temping, if that even exists here, and they only had night stocker positions open, and I –

Pause.

And I just wanted to work – here.

They stand awkwardly for a moment.

CHRIS. The health benefits are good.

Pause.

I mean Costco, they have good benefits. The health plans are pretty good.

JAKE. Well there's no treatment for Huntington's so it doesn't really matter.

CHRIS. Really?

JAKE. I mean there's pills.

CHRIS. Do they help?

JAKE. Sort of. They don't really cure it, they just slow it down.

Pause.

CHRIS. Does it ever / go away?

JAKE. I'm gonna be dead before I'm thirty, pretty much for certain.

Silence. JAKE *stares at his feet.*

(*Re. the mess.*) Is there like a broom or / dustpan – ?

CHRIS. Oh, yeah I can – Here I can get it.

JAKE. If you just tell me where / it is –

CHRIS. No, I'll – I'll get it.

CHRIS exits. Silence apart from the sound of stocking and machinery in the background.

JAKE is about to go back to shelving when his phone starts vibrating. He takes it out of his pocket, looks at it.

It continues to buzz, he looks at it, not moving. CHRIS re-enters with a broom and dustpan.

Don't let Janet see you with that. She goes ballistic about the phones.

JAKE quickly turns off the phone, puts it back in his pocket.

JAKE. I just – forgot to turn it off.

CHRIS. She caught me texting on the clock a few months ago and I swear she almost punched me in the face.

CHRIS starts to clean up the mess.

Product loss isn't a big deal. Janet's actually pretty cool about the little stuff. Just don't do it with anything expensive.

JAKE. Sure.

CHRIS. This guy TJ ran a forklift over a box of iPads a while back. It was so fucking hilarious.

JAKE. Did he do it on purpose?

CHRIS. Said he didn't, but it happened like the day after Janet didn't give him a raise after his eval, so. He got fired pretty quick.

JAKE tentatively goes back to stocking, not looking at CHRIS.

Pause.

Hey.

JAKE looks at him.

I won't tell anyone, okay?

Pause.

Carrie does all the scheduling, I know her pretty well, so I'll make sure we do our shifts together. You need to take a break or whatever, you let me know. Just don't – Try not to break a lot of stuff.

CHRIS *smiles at him, continues to clean up the mess.* JAKE *stocks.*

So you like – ? But why are you here?

JAKE. What do you mean?

CHRIS. If you just wanna see the ocean, why'd you stop in Clarkston, why work here?

Pause. JAKE *continues to stock, shelving large plastic tubs of cheese puffs.*

JAKE. I just felt like – I wanted to stop for a while.

Pause.

And I mean I thought maybe this would be good for me, I've never really had a job like this, like a – *real* job.

CHRIS. Huh.

JAKE. I mean if you think about it, all these stores like Costco in towns like this, hundreds of miles in between one another – maybe this is like the new west.

CHRIS. That's like the most depressing thing I've heard in a *while.*

JAKE. I don't think so. Maybe we're like the last American pioneers.

CHRIS. Cheese puffs go on the bottom.

JAKE. Oh.

JAKE *moves the tubs to the correct row.*

CHRIS *finishes cleaning up the mess, starts to sweep up the popcorn kernels with the dustpan and brush.*

Anyway I just needed to get away for a while I guess.

CHRIS. Sure.

JAKE. *And* I just got dumped.

CHRIS. That sucks.

JAKE. Yeah. I got the diagnosis, and a few months later he realizes we don't have a long-term future together so he just fucking – Anyway. Asshole.

CHRIS tenses up for a brief moment, keeps cleaning. JAKE senses his discomfort.

Oh, sorry.

CHRIS. No, it's [fine] –

JAKE. I don't even think about it anymore, I – I've been out since I was like fifteen, both of my parents were like *hyper* okay with it, like to the point where it was a little annoying actually, but – Anyway I don't really think about it very much. But I guess out here it's a bigger deal.

CHRIS. Nah, it's fine.

JAKE. I hope that wasn't weird of me to –

CHRIS. No, really, it's – It's really fine.

Pause.

A brief moment of recognition between the two of them. CHRIS quickly ends it, finishes sweeping up the popcorn kernels. He motions offstage.

I'm just gonna –

JAKE. Oh sure.

CHRIS is about to exit, then turns back to JAKE.

CHRIS. It's actually not a bad place, you know?

Pause.

Snake River is really beautiful, you can take boats down it when it's nice out. You'll get used to the smell of the paper mill after a few days.

Pause.

I think you'll like it here.

Scene Two

JAKE, *alone, sitting in the parking lot, his cellphone in his hand. He looks at it for a moment, then makes a call.*

JAKE. Hi, Dad.

Short pause.

Okay please calm down, please – I'm sorry, I know you've been calling, I'm – Yes, I'm *fine*, I'm taking my meds, I'm safe.

JAKE *stands up, paces aimlessly.*

No, I'm – I'm not in Connecticut. I went – West.

Short pause.

Okay, look, I'm sorry for just leaving like that. And I understand that you're worried, and I know that this is selfish of me, I realize that, but please believe me when I say I *had* to do this, I had to do *something*, I had to –

JAKE *has an involuntary movement in his leg, he nearly trips and falls. He steadies himself for a second, takes a few breaths. He touches his leg, moves it a little bit, begins to calm down.*

No, I'm – I'm still here.

Pause.

Okay, I'm not calling to tell you I'm coming home, I'm just calling to let you know that I'm safe.

Pause.

I mean I'm not sure I *am* coming back, I –

JAKE *sits back down. Pause.*

I don't know how to answer that, is *anyone* ever happy?

Pause.

Look, I have to – I have to go. I'll call you.

JAKE *hangs up, looking at his phone.*

Scene Three

Much later, at the far edge of the parking lot, near the river.

JAKE *and* CHRIS *stand at a distance from one another.* JAKE *has been drinking.* CHRIS *looks around nervously.*

Awkward silence.

CHRIS. Hey.

JAKE. Hey.

   Pause.

CHRIS. You okay?

JAKE. Fine.

CHRIS. You've been drinking?

JAKE. I'm not drunk.

CHRIS. It's okay, I don't care if you're / drunk.

JAKE. I'm not drunk.

CHRIS. Okay.

JAKE. Sometimes it's – The chorea, it helps with it.

CHRIS. The what?

JAKE. It's like a symptom of the [disease] – These involuntary movements, I was telling you before.

CHRIS. Oh, yeah.

   CHRIS *looks around nervously.*

JAKE. No one's gonna see us.

CHRIS. I'm not worried about that.

   Pause.

   Look I'd invite you back to my place but it's – You have a room or something?

JAKE. I'm staying in the hotel across the street.

CHRIS. Can we go there?

JAKE looks out to the river.

JAKE. I kind of like the river. I like being by the river.

CHRIS. My truck is over there.

JAKE. No one can see us here. And no one's left in the store anyway.

CHRIS. Benji's around. The security guy?

JAKE. He's like a hundred. Plus he'd have to circle around the fence to see us –

CHRIS. I just don't want to get in / trouble with –

JAKE. Look we don't have to do this.

Pause.

CHRIS. No, I –

I wanna do this.

JAKE takes a tentative step toward him. CHRIS is obviously nervous.

Silence.

(*Dirty.*) So you want it?

Pause.

JAKE. What?

CHRIS (*really bad at being dirty*). I'm asking if you want it. Do you want what I have.

JAKE. . . . Sure.

CHRIS. It's ready for you.

Awkward pause.

I'm talking about my / penis.

JAKE. Sure yep I know.

Finally, CHRIS goes to him. He stands face to face with him. They look at one another.

JAKE *reaches for* CHRIS' *belt,* CHRIS *exhales, his shoulders falling.*

JAKE *fiddles with the belt buckle.*

I can't get the buckle.

CHRIS *looks.*

CHRIS. No you have to like / open the –

JAKE. This is like the biggest buckle I've ever / seen –

CHRIS. Are you gonna make fun of me / or are you – ?

JAKE. Sorry but I don't know how any self-respecting –

A car horn in the distance. CHRIS *jumps back, looking toward the noise, terrified.*

Whoa, calm down –

CHRIS. Sorry, sorry –

JAKE. It's just – It's the other side of the store, no one can see us.

CHRIS. Sorry.

Pause.

JAKE. Have you never done this before?

Pause.

CHRIS. I mean I've been with guys.

JAKE. Yeah.

CHRIS. But just not – Not like this.

Pause, embarrassed.

Fuck.

CHRIS *looks away. Silence.*

Look sorry this is weird, I'm being weird, we don't have to –

JAKE *goes to him, kissing him. It's awkward at first,* CHRIS *doesn't know what to do. Finally he relaxes into it. It lasts for just a few moments. They look at one another.*

Pause.

You taste / like –

JAKE. It's root beer schnapps, I'm / sorry.

CHRIS. It's really disgusting.

JAKE. Yeah.

Pause.

CHRIS. Do you do this – a lot?

JAKE. Are you asking me if I'm a slut?

CHRIS. No, I just – I don't know / what to –

JAKE. We can do whatever you want. I mean not *whatever*, but – You know.

Pause.

CHRIS *goes to him.* JAKE *is about to reach for* CHRIS' *belt when* CHRIS *gets down on his knees. He begins to undo* JAKE's *belt.* JAKE *tenses up.*

CHRIS *undoes his belt, is about to unbutton his pants when* JAKE *suddenly turns away from him, takes a few steps away from him, becoming upset.*

Pause.

Shit.

JAKE *buttons his belt.*

CHRIS. I'm sorry, I / didn't mean –

JAKE. No, it's – It's me.

Pause.

I thought I could do this.

CHRIS. It's cool –

JAKE. *No it's not it's –*

> *Pause.*

> I thought I could handle it and then I got nervous and I drank these disgusting root beer shots to calm myself down and now I just feel sick.

> *Pause.*

CHRIS. Wait are you – ? Have you never done this before?

JAKE. Look, to be honest up until now I've been borderline puritanical, I wouldn't even have sex with my boyfriend until we'd been dating for – I've just always been that way and I thought maybe *one fucking time* I could just –

> JAKE *looks out toward the river. He sits down on the asphalt.*

> You have this idea in your head of the person you could be – but then it turns out you're just the same asshole you've always been.

> *Silence.*

CHRIS. Look, it's – It's no big deal, I mean I don't know if I could have done this either –

JAKE. You know back in 1805 William Clark was camping, *right here*. Right where this parking lot is now.

> *Pause, looking.*

> They'd been traveling for like a year and a half. And they camped here. The confluence of the Clearwater and Snake rivers. They were like – the *first people* to see it.

> *Pause.* CHRIS *looks.*

CHRIS. I mean except for like *all* the Indians.

JAKE. Right.

> *Pause.*

> I'm not racist.

CHRIS. No I know.

Pause.

Also didn't like a lot of French trappers and / Spanish – ?

JAKE. *Point is*, they just – I mean they were like *doing* something.

Pause.

I wonder if they knew then that someday there wouldn't be any more pioneers. That like two hundred years later pretty much no matter where you live in America, you have a car and can drive to Costco.

CHRIS. I mean that's what they wanted, right? Make it so America reached this far. Make it so people could live out here and be comfortable and happy.

JAKE. Are *you* comfortable and happy?

Silence.

CHRIS. Look, I'm gonna [go home] – Let's forget this happened, I don't want it to be weird at work or / anything –

JAKE. How deep do you think it is?

CHRIS. What?

JAKE. The river, right here. How deep do you think it is?

CHRIS *looks out toward the river.*

CHRIS. I don't know. I mean pretty deep. Toward the middle – thirty feet? More? I'm sort of guessing.

JAKE. Huh.

JAKE *stands up, his eyes fixed on the water.*

CHRIS. Are you / okay?

JAKE. If I walked into it would you wait an hour or so before you called the police?

Pause.

CHRIS. Wait, what?

JAKE. Like just wait a while so you know that I'm…

CHRIS. Wait, you're gonna – ?

Pause.

JAKE (*oddly unsure*). I think so?

JAKE *looks out to the river. CHRIS watches him. Silence.*

CHRIS. This isn't –

Pause.

This is totally unfair.

JAKE. I'm sorry.

CHRIS. I mean this is – I mean this is, like – You're asking for help, right?

JAKE *looks at him.*

JAKE. No. I really don't want that. I really, really don't / want your help.

CHRIS. *Well then I don't know what* – I just don't know what you expect me to do here –

JAKE. I know I've just met you and this is awkward and I'm sorry but I think the best thing you could do for me right now is watch me go into the water and make sure I don't come out. Make sure I don't fail at it like I do at everything else.

Pause.

Like twenty minutes?

JAKE *looks back out to the water. He takes a step toward the river. CHRIS takes a step toward him.*

CHRIS. Wait, you –

JAKE *stops, still looking at the river. CHRIS thinks, changes tactic.*

Alright then, fine. Do it.

JAKE *looks at him.*

Go for it. I'll make sure you don't come out. Go ahead.

Pause.

JAKE. Okay.

JAKE *starts walking toward the river.*

CHRIS. *NO WAIT JESUS –*

JAKE *stops, looks at* CHRIS.

I thought that would work for some reason.

Short pause.

I'm a moron.

JAKE *smiles despite himself.* CHRIS *is heartened by it.*

Pause.

I mean is it – ? Is it because of the disease, the – ?

JAKE. No, it's – I mean that's part of it, sure, but the Huntington's just like – What's that phrase? It – put it 'into stark relief,' that's it. It put it into stark relief.

Pause, looking at CHRIS.

I mean have you ever been like *certain* that nothing you do is ever going to amount to anything? Have you ever looked at your life and been one hundred percent certain that when you die the world will be *no different*? I have never made, and will never make, any discernible contribution to society. I have a degree in *Post-Colonial Gender Studies.*

Silence.

CHRIS. You know I wanna be a writer.

JAKE. A writer?

CHRIS. Yeah, like – Fiction writer. I write short stories. Maybe a novel someday, hopefully.

JAKE. Huh.

CHRIS. Yeah, you know the Iowa Writers Workshop? Have you ever heard of it?

JAKE. Maybe.

CHRIS. It's a masters degree program, like the best in the country for fiction writing. I applied this year. And I think I have a good chance, actually, I wrote the head of the program an email and she actually responded, she said that she was 'looking forward' to reading my application.

JAKE. That's – good.

CHRIS. Anyway, I just think that – I mean like if I write something, like I write something that gets published, and – I mean I don't have to get famous or rich or anything, I just think if someday someone in a bookshop or a library or whatever pulls out my book and reads one of my stories and *likes* it then I – I mean then I've done something.

Pause.

I'm just saying, I think there are like different ways to contribute. To society.

Silence. JAKE *looks out toward the river.*

JAKE. It's a terrible time to be alive. There's just nothing left to discover.

Silence.

I'm gonna just sit here for a while.

CHRIS. Yeah, me too.

CHRIS *sits down next to* JAKE.

JAKE. You really don't have / to –

CHRIS. Sun's gonna come up soon, it's nice.

Pause. JAKE *looks out to the river, feels a gust of wind. He smiles a little.*

JAKE (*quietly*). 'A cool morning wind from the east.'

CHRIS. What?

JAKE. It's – I was reading some of the journals earlier. William Clark's journals from when they got to the Snake River, around here. It starts like, 'a cool morning wind from the east.'

CHRIS. Huh.

Pause. JAKE *thinks.*

JAKE. 'Had examined and dried all our clothes and other articles. Laid out a small assortment of articles as those Indians were fond of to trade with for provisions.'

CHRIS *watches him.* JAKE *closes his eyes.*

'Captain Lewis getting much better. Several Indians visit us from different tribes.'

Pause.

'Our hunters killed nothing today. Nothing to eat except a little dried fish.'

Pause.

'Warm evening.'

CHRIS *continues to watch him.* JAKE *takes a deep breath.*

Scene Four

The next night, in the parking lot near the store. TRISHA, *wearing a Denny's uniform, nervously smokes a cigarette, holds a tote bag.*

CHRIS *looks at her, keeping his distance. A silence between them.*

CHRIS. We gonna do this every week?

TRISHA. You tell me, hon.

TRISHA *stubs out her cigarette, extends the tote bag toward* CHRIS.

I got you some groceries.

CHRIS. I don't –

Pause.

Thank you, but I don't need groceries, I've told / you that.

TRISHA. It's just a few little things, the tuna you like and / the –

CHRIS. I don't want you buying things for me, you need to save your / money –

TRISHA. I'd really just like to feel like your mom? Just once in a while?

Pause.

CHRIS. When I said I didn't want to see you for a while, I meant that I needed some / time –

TRISHA. Well I've been keeping my distance, haven't I? You said you needed space, I gave you space, I just don't know why –

Pause.

Come back home, Chris? Please?

Pause.

CHRIS. Have you – used at all?

TRISHA. Chris –

CHRIS. Tell me the truth, since I left have / you – ?

TRISHA. Nothing, not once. That's six months. You know that.

Pause.

CHRIS. That's good.

TRISHA. Yeah, it's – It's good, I'm just the same boring old mom I was when you were little.

(*Extending the tote bag.*) Here, just – Let me feel like your mother for one goddam minute.

CHRIS *moves to her, takes the tote bag.*

CHRIS. Thanks.

CHRIS *looks inside the tote bag. He reaches in, pulls out a small worn stuffed dog. He looks at it.*

TRISHA (*smiling*). You didn't take Clancy with you, just thought he could – He was your favorite, right? I mean more / than –

CHRIS. Please stop bringing me stuff from home, I don't –

Pause.

Yeah, he was my favorite.

TRISHA. You staying with anyone, you – ? I mean are you – *seeing* someone?

CHRIS. Mom.

TRISHA. I just don't know where you're staying, I don't know what kind of people you're going home to –

CHRIS. I'm not – I'm not seeing anyone.

Pause.

TRISHA. You just – You be careful, you hear me?

CHRIS. I know.

TRISHA. Around here, you don't know what – I mean you just don't know how people are / gonna react –

CHRIS. I said I know, Mom.

TRISHA. I knew this kid in high school, he got it real bad once, was at the Mill Tavern downtown and these guys – he ended up in the hospital for a couple / nights –

CHRIS. *I know Mom, you've* [told me this already] –

Pause.

I gotta clock in.

CHRIS *turns to exit.*

TRISHA. Jesus, Chris, would you please just gimme a chance? I just wanna talk to you.

Pause.

Listen, I told those guys they can't come around the house anymore. I'm serious, it's done, I told them after you left – they aren't allowed to be in my life anymore. You were right, they were bad for me, I just couldn't [see it] –

Pause.

Look I'm not saying I didn't have a bad year, I'm not saying that I've made all the right choices. But I'm *better*, you know? I'm just asking you to – *acknowledge* that I'm doing better. I'm here because I don't know where else I can talk to you, I'm damn near ready to follow you home at night just to make / sure you –

CHRIS. Do *not* follow me home –

TRISHA. *I'm not gonna follow you home* –

CHRIS. Look, do you just need money?

Pause.

TRISHA. Excuse me?

CHRIS. If you need some help this month, I can get you a couple hundred bucks, just please stop showing up / here and –

TRISHA. I *don't need money*, Chris, I – Is that what you really think this is about?

CHRIS. Well?

Pause.

TRISHA *stares at him.*

TRISHA. Rent's paid for the month, fridge is full. Trevor bumped me back up to forty hours a week at Denny's. We've been busy, the car show in town. Tips are good.

Pause.

CHRIS. That's – good.

TRISHA. Yeah. It is.

Pause.

CHRIS. I just didn't – I wasn't sure if it was like two summers ago, I / didn't –

TRISHA. That happened one time, and I paid you back. I paid you back, right?

CHRIS. Yeah, you / paid me –

TRISHA. You think that's the worst I've ever seen?

Pause.

When you were nine or ten, when I lost my job at the paper mill? Your dad hadn't been in town for months, my parents said they'd only help me out with money if I sent you to live with them for good. Could you imagine that, you growing up with those people?

Pause.

I started working sixty hours a week, full-time at the Albertsons', part-time janitor at the hospital, all so we could keep a place where you had your own bedroom and you could still go to camp that summer. When you were at that camp I was mostly eating expired stuff the Albertsons was throwing away.

Pause.

CHRIS. Why did you – ? I didn't have to go to camp, I –

TRISHA. You loved it there. I'd go and see you on the weekends and you'd tell me about hiking up into the woods, swimming in that lake. You said you could name the constellations, you were so proud.

Pause.

CHRIS *looks at her.*

Listen, Chris – I know that it's been bad, it's not surprising you up and left like that. But I'm better now and it doesn't have to be like this is all I'm saying. We don't need to be living apart. We're a team, we always have been. We need each other, right?

Pause.

CHRIS. I don't know, I –

Pause.

I just need some time.

TRISHA. Right, okay. I'll give you time.

Pause.

I can come by again tomorrow? Just to say hi?

Pause.

CHRIS. My shift tomorrow starts at ten.

Pause.

TRISHA. These night shifts aren't good for you.

CHRIS. Well it's money.

TRISHA. You remember a few years ago when I used to work nights? I don't think I slept for two years.

CHRIS. You didn't sleep for two years because you were always on meth, Mom.

Silence.

TRISHA. If you come by Denny's after work I can get you a free breakfast. Whatever you want. I know you don't like the food that much but it's free.

Pause.

CHRIS. I like the / pancakes.

TRISHA. Pancakes, I know it. You come by and I'll get you all the pancakes you want.

CHRIS. Let's just meet here tomorrow before my shift. Okay?

TRISHA. Okay.

> *Pause.*

> TRISHA *moves toward him, her arms outstretched for a hug.*

> CHRIS *looks at her for a moment, not moving.*

CHRIS. I'll see you later.

> CHRIS *exits.* TRISHA *watches him go. She lowers her arms.*

Scene Five

Camping Gear: Tents and Tent Accessories.

A shelf littered with boxed-up tents of different sizes. One of the boxes has been opened, the box has the word 'DISPLAY' in large letters written on the side of it. CHRIS *is unloading a palette, having just started.*

JAKE enters, hurried and disheveled.

He looks at CHRIS. CHRIS *gives him an awkward smile, avoiding eye contact.*

JAKE. I'm really sorry –

CHRIS. It's okay.

JAKE. I didn't realize how late it / had gotten –

CHRIS. I'm not your boss, Jake, it's [fine] – Janet's not too strict about it anyway, as long as you put in the hours.

JAKE. Okay. Cool. Sorry.

> *Pause.*

> CHRIS *looks away.*

CHRIS. We, uh. We need to put one of the tents together for the display and shelve all / the –

JAKE. I can do the tent.

Pause.

CHRIS. You know how to [put together a tent] – ?

JAKE. Yeah, sure.

    CHRIS *resumes shelving.* JAKE *goes into the box, takes out some of the parts, realizes he does not in fact know how to put together a tent.*

    CHRIS *watches him.*

CHRIS. You can start with the –

JAKE. I got it.

    Pause.

    JAKE *takes the tent cover, stands back, and unfurls it onto the floor, trying to make it seem like he knows what he's doing.*

    Look, um.

    I was drunk?

    Short pause.

CHRIS. Well, yeah.

JAKE. It's just been a hard – I got the diagnosis like six months ago, and my boyfriend broke up with me like four months after that, so it's just been – rough.

    Pause.

CHRIS. You know there are hotlines and prevention centers and people you can / talk to –

JAKE. No, I don't – I mean I was just drunk.

CHRIS. So you weren't serious about it?

    Pause.

JAKE. Nah.

CHRIS *looks at him, knows he's lying.* JAKE *looks away, pulls the tent poles out of the box. He looks at them. He begins putting them together.*

Was that your mom?

CHRIS. What?

JAKE. The lady in the parking lot.

Pause.

CHRIS *looks away.*

CHRIS. Yeah, she – Yeah.

Pause.

JAKE. My mom was on pain pills for like *most* of my childhood.

Pause.

CHRIS *looks at him.*

She fell down some concrete stairs when I was little, shattered her kneecap. After that she was always on pain pills, and for years it was like I didn't know what version of her I was gonna get when I came home from school.

CHRIS. / What?

JAKE. My parents got divorced when I twelve and my mom finally went to rehab, now she likes to say that she was only on the pills because my dad was making her unhappy, which is complete bullshit, and now all she talks about is her fucking chakras and expelling toxins and –

CHRIS. Wait, you were listening to us?

JAKE *looks at him, stops working.*

JAKE. *No*, I just – Look I just heard her say like *one thing* about / getting clean –

CHRIS. That's really not okay.

JAKE. I wasn't like *listening*, I was just –

CHRIS. I'm serious, don't eavesdrop on me and my fucking mom.

JAKE. Calm down – I mean you were having the conversation in a *public place*, it's not like I was –

Pause.

Wow. Okay.

Pause.

JAKE *is taken aback, he goes back to the tent poles. He is awkwardly putting one of them together without threading it through first.*

Are you not *out* or something?

CHRIS. How about we just work, how about that?

JAKE. Fine. Jesus.

CHRIS *goes back to stocking, annoyed.* JAKE *rolls his eyes, goes back to the tent. The pole is now unreasonably long, he struggles to thread it through the tent.*

CHRIS. Christ, just let me do it.

JAKE *gives up, hands him the pole.* CHRIS *starts taking it apart, then threads it through the tent correctly.* JAKE *starts stocking the shelves.*

I just don't want to be like *responsible* for you or anything.

Pause.

JAKE. What?

CHRIS. Like I just – I don't think it's fair that I have to be the one that makes sure you don't [kill yourself] –

Pause.

JAKE (*cold*). You don't need to worry.

CHRIS. I'm not trying to be insensitive.

JAKE. Right.

CHRIS. I'm just saying I can't really – I mean I barely know you –

JAKE. Yeah well I guess since I didn't suck your dick last night we're not –

CHRIS *drops the tent, turning on* JAKE *angrily.*

CHRIS. *Stop.*

JAKE *backs away from him.*

JAKE. *Jesus Christ…*

Pause.

CHRIS *regains himself.*

CHRIS. Just shut up, okay?

Pause.

JAKE. Are you really *that far* in the closet?

CHRIS. Jake.

JAKE. What, you think we're gonna get arrested or / something?

CHRIS. What I think is you're not in fucking Connecticut.

Pause.

I am 'out' to the people I *want* to be out to. So just [shut up] –

CHRIS *goes back to setting up the tent.* JAKE *looks at him for a moment, then goes back to work as well.*

Pause.

You know Lewis and Clark were sort of douchebags, right?

JAKE *looks at him.* CHRIS *continues to pitch the tent.*

JAKE. What?

CHRIS. I'm just saying, they – I mean I was reading some stuff online earlier today, it's not like they were – I mean there had been plenty of people who had already been out here, it's not like they were like the *first* people / who saw –

JAKE. I didn't mean they were literally the / first –

CHRIS. And they would approach all these Indian tribes and give them some stupid speech about how they – like, how Thomas Jefferson was their new *chief* or something? And Clark had a fucking *slave* with him? Did you know that?

JAKE. *Yes*, I knew that, / I –

CHRIS. I don't know why we have to think they were so fucking *noble* or whatever, they were just sort of glorified colonialists claiming land for America that was 'sold' to us by France even though they –

JAKE. Chris, what are you doing?

CHRIS looks at him, then goes back to working on the tent. He struggles to pitch it by himself. Silence.

JAKE slowly goes to CHRIS, helping him with the tent. CHRIS looks at him for a brief moment, then looks away. They pitch the tent together.

Finally:

CHRIS. You know I really do care about her.

Pause.

JAKE. Maybe you should tell her that.

Pause.

And I know they were kind of assholes. Lewis and Clark. And I know Clark had a slave, and that's –

Pause.

I just like the idea of them more than what they actually were I guess.

They secure the second pole, the tent is pitched.

CHRIS. There.

Pause.

JAKE. Looks okay.

CHRIS. Sort of.

Pause.

CHRIS *takes out the tent cover, handing it to* JAKE. JAKE *starts to put the cover on the tent.*

CHRIS *looks at the box.*

Pause.

It wasn't even made here. Manufactured in Shenzhen.

JAKE. That's a city?

CHRIS. Yeah, in China. I've read about it. This city that's nothing but industry, built really quickly. Forty years ago it was a fishing village and now it's like this monster.

JAKE. Huh.

JAKE *has some involuntary movement in his hand, he struggles to attach the tent cover.*

Goddammit…

CHRIS *sees, going to him. He steadies* JAKE*'s hand, allowing him to secure the tent cover. They look at one another briefly.*

CHRIS *lets go of* JAKE*'s hand.*

Pause.

They both stand back, looking at the tent.

Pause.

It's a shitty tent.

CHRIS. Yeah it doesn't look very good.

Scene Six

Days later, after their shift, very early morning. JAKE *and* CHRIS *are sitting in the parking lot with their backpacks.* CHRIS *is reading from a notebook.*

CHRIS (*reading*). 'The fog washed over his boat in gigantic waves of blank space, deleting everything around him farther than fifteen feet. And as he reached for an oar to paddle himself back to the dock, he suddenly realized that the steady bleating of the foghorn had ceased. He hadn't – '

JAKE. Wait, is this – ? It's scary?

CHRIS. Well, yeah, it's / kind of –

JAKE. Is this like a ghost story?

CHRIS. I mean there aren't any *ghosts* in it –

JAKE. But it's like scary, right?

CHRIS. I mean, sure, it's scary, but that's not like the point / of the –

JAKE. I just don't do well with scary stuff.

CHRIS. I can stop.

JAKE. Yeah maybe you should. No keep going. Sorry. Shut up.

Pause.

CHRIS *goes back to reading.*

CHRIS. '…he suddenly realized that the steady bleating of the / foghorn – '

JAKE. Wait and you realize this is like *where I grew up*. A coast, with the cold, and the fog? You're writing about where I grew up.

CHRIS. Oh, yeah, I mean it could be a lot of places, / but –

JAKE. I thought you've never seen the ocean?

CHRIS. I haven't. I just like writing about it.

JAKE. Huh.

Pause.

I keep interrupting sorry keep going.

CHRIS *goes back to reading.*

CHRIS. '…he suddenly realized that the steady bleating of the foghorn had ceased. He hadn't noticed the precise moment it had stopped, but he suddenly felt its absence like he was missing a life-preserver. The idea that he had suddenly floated out to sea far enough that he wasn't able to hear the foghorn was ridiculous, so he managed to convince himself that something had gone wrong with it, not him. But it wasn't until he grabbed a paddle that he realized – without the foghorn, he wasn't entirely sure what direction land was – '

JAKE *groans a bit.*

You realize I just made this up.

JAKE. No I mean it's good, I like it. When I grew up I was *petrified* of the ocean, so.

CHRIS. You grew up on the water and you were scared of it?

JAKE. When I was a kid I almost drowned.

CHRIS. Oh, wow.

JAKE. Yeah. And the thing about drowning is that it doesn't look anything like it does on TV, you don't yell and thrash around, you just – My dad was like ten feet away from me, didn't even realize. Lifeguard finally saw what was going on, saved me.

Pause.

CHRIS. You want me to keep going?

JAKE. Oh yeah of course, I'm just – I'm just ridiculous, I'm a mess. Keep going.

Pause.

CHRIS (*resumes reading*). 'But being reasonably sure the dock was behind him a hundred or so feet, he reached for a paddle and put it into the water. In what felt like less than a second, the paddle was gone.'

JAKE *groans again.*

'The moment had gone by so quickly that he had barely had time to process it. But he could have sworn there was some subtle force other than gravity that had pulled the oar down into the opaque waters.'

JAKE. Oh god.

JAKE *tenses up, hugging his knees.* CHRIS *enjoys his discomfort, taking it as a compliment.*

CHRIS. 'Pushing the thought out of his head as quickly as possible, he leaned over the side of the boat, putting his hand into the water, hoping that the oar was floating gently beneath the surface. The fog grew thicker and wetter and he stared down at the water, moving his hand back and forth. Then, leaning further over the edge of the boat – '

JAKE. / *Eeeee* –

CHRIS. ' – he stuck his hand farther into the water when, like a pair of flashlights being switched on, two bright-yellow human eyes appeared in the water staring up / at him – '

JAKE (*standing up*). Okay nope nope nope sorry nope.

CHRIS (*smiling*). Sorry –

JAKE. Seriously stop reading.

CHRIS. I'm stopping, I stopped –

JAKE. Don't laugh at me it's not funny.

CHRIS. I'm not!

JAKE. That's like –

Pause.

Okay you managed to put like *all of my fears ever* into one story.

CHRIS. That's neat.

JAKE. No it isn't! I have to go back to my dark empty hotel room after this.

CHRIS *picks up a pipe that's sitting next to him, offers it to* JAKE.

CHRIS. You want the last hit?

JAKE. *No*, I am – I am *good*. I haven't smoked weed in months, I'm sort of freaking out.

CHRIS. I don't have to read the rest –

JAKE. No, I want – I'm sorry, I know I'm being annoying, I want to hear the rest, but could you – Just skip the scary stuff?

Pause.

CHRIS. Seriously?

JAKE. It's fucking *dark* and I don't want to think about two flashlight eyes / or whatever – !

CHRIS. But it's like – I mean it's a scary story, I don't know / how to –

JAKE. Okay whatever just read it. Shut up. Read it read it read it.

JAKE *sits back down, hugging his knees.* CHRIS *looks at his notebook.*

CHRIS. Okay.

(*Reads.*) 'The eyes remained under the surface, unblinking, looking straight at him, and as he continued to stare back he realized the eyes had a deep sense of grief in them, a grief he recognized as his own. Suddenly the eyes weren't shocking and unexplainable, they were entirely recognizable, almost mundane, as familiar as his own eyes looking back at him in the mirror every morning. Suddenly these eyes, though jaundiced yellow and incandescent, were his own.'

JAKE *listens, unmoving.* CHRIS *looks at him.*

You okay?

JAKE. Yeah, I'm –

Pause.

Keep going.

JAKE *sits near him, listening intently as he watches the river in front of him.*

CHRIS (*reading*). 'The grief that he recognized in those eyes was the grief he felt every night going home to his empty apartment, the grief he felt when he would drive his aging pick-up to work, the grief he felt almost every moment of every day, the grief that somehow only seemed to go away when he was in his boat, on the water, in the fog. The haze continued to roll in, gaining a thickness that seemed impossible, and soon the ocean itself was shielded in white, and he could barely make out the end of his boat. As the whiteness closed in around him, covering his feet, then his legs, then his torso, the only thing that remained visible in the void were the two constant eyes staring up at him. Slowly, he no longer felt his boat beneath him, he no longer felt the clothes on his body. His five senses had been stripped from him one by one, the glowing yellow eyes his last connection to the world around him. And just as he had his last thought – the briefest thought of a smile – the eyes were extinguished.'

Silence. CHRIS *puts the notebook away.* JAKE *looks at him.*

That's it.

Pause.

I mean it's just like a tiny short story. It's like my shortest. I think the last paragraph is sort of dumb, I / should –

JAKE. That was crazy.

Pause.

I mean it was good, it was – It was good.

CHRIS. Thanks.

JAKE. It was crazy though. The end is crazy.

Pause.

What's it about?

CHRIS *thinks.*

CHRIS. I mean I don't know. I don't know if it's about anything.

JAKE. Huh.

CHRIS. I guess when I write I don't try to have like one single point that I'm trying to make. I'm not trying to give a moral or something.

Silence.

JAKE. Wait – is it about suicide?

CHRIS. It's brand new, I don't know. Maybe it's too weird.

Pause.

JAKE. I think it's really good, I think you're gonna get in.

CHRIS. Really?

JAKE. Yeah totally.

CHRIS. It's really hard to get into. We'll see.

Pause.

So what do you wanna do?

JAKE. Like, now?

CHRIS. I mean like – I mean what do you want to do in the future, after you go see the ocean?

Pause.

JAKE. I don't know. I mean I've only got like eight years, maybe, that's what they said. But toward the end it's not like it's gonna be easy for me to get around or –

CHRIS. Sorry, we don't have to talk / about it –

JAKE. Nah, it's – It's fine. I mean it's a degenerative disease, so it'll take a while, but. Eventually it's – It's not gonna be pretty. I'll lose control of my limbs, won't be able to walk, difficulty swallowing, talking, and – I'll start to lose memories, they'll fragment and distort and then eventually full-blown dementia, and –

Pause.

Basically my body is gonna forget how to be alive.

Silence. Finally, JAKE *jumps up.*

Okay, another one!

CHRIS. What?

JAKE. Read me another story. I'm ready to be freaked out again.

CHRIS. Oh, naw –

JAKE. C'mon.

CHRIS. Why don't *you* read me something?

JAKE. Me?

CHRIS. Yeah, read me something from the journals, William Clark's journals. You've been reading them, right?

JAKE. I mean, I'm always reading them.

Pause.

I don't think you'd like find them interesting.

CHRIS. C'mon, I wanna hear. Let's hear what your great-great-whatever-grandpa had to say.

JAKE. Cousin.

CHRIS. Whatever.

Pause.

JAKE *opens up his bag, takes out a worn paperback book.*

JAKE. You wanna hear about anything in particular?

CHRIS. You said he wrote some while he was around here, right? Read me that part.

JAKE. Okay then. Early October, 1805.

JAKE thumbs through the book a bit, lands on a page.

(*Reads.*) 'Had all our horses, thirty-eight in number, collected and branded. Cut off their foretop and / delivered – '

CHRIS. What's 'foretop'?

JAKE shrugs.

JAKE (*reads*). ' – and delivered them to the two brothers and one son of one of the chiefs who intents to' blah blah blah, stuff about horses…

(*Skims.*) 'Captain Lewis and myself ate a supper of roots boiled, which filled us so full of wind that we were scarcely able to breathe all night.'

CHRIS. It really says that?

JAKE. Yeah, diet was a big deal to them. It was like half the battle of being out here.

CHRIS. Huh.

JAKE. 'I am very sick tonight, pain in stomach and the bowels owing to my diet. It is certainly the effects of my diet last night.'

CHRIS (*laughs*). Okay.

JAKE. 'Tonight Captain Lewis and myself ate a supper of roots boiled, which swelled us in such a manner that we were scarcely able to breathe for several hours – '

CHRIS. Well stop eating the fuckin' boiled roots.

They both start giggling, both fairly high by this point and getting silly.

JAKE. 'Several squars came with fish and roots which we purchased of them for beads – '

CHRIS. WHY ARE YOU BUYING MORE ROOTS?!

Their giggling increases, becoming a laughing fit.

JAKE. Okay, okay –

They calm down, breathing.

CHRIS. This is what you just sit and read all day?

JAKE. Yeah, I guess.

CHRIS. And you like it?

JAKE. Sure, it's – I love it.

CHRIS. What's your favorite part?

JAKE continues to calm down, thinks.

JAKE. I mean everybody likes, 'Ocean in View! O! The Joy!' It's what he said when he finally saw the Pacific. It's like printed on a quarter I think. It's famous.

CHRIS. That's your favorite?

JAKE. I guess.

Pause.

I mean I don't know. I like a lot of it.

CHRIS. I haven't thought about it very much, growing up here, but – I mean thinking that we're sitting here right now, like right where they were two hundred years ago…

Pause.

JAKE thinks for a second. He looks toward the river, thinking.

CHRIS. What?

JAKE looks around for another moment.

JAKE. Huh.

CHRIS. What?

JAKE. I just realized, they – They weren't here. We're on the Washington side, they were on the Idaho side. I didn't even – I didn't even realize it until just now.

Pause.

They weren't here.

CHRIS. Huh.

Pause.

I mean you can go to the other side, it's really easy, the bridge is just like a three-minute drive down there.

JAKE *continues to look at the river.*

A very long silence. Finally:

Are you / okay?

JAKE. 'I took two men and set out in a small canoe and ascended the Columbia River ten miles to an island near the starboard.'

(*Closing his eyes.*) 'The number of dead salmon on the shores and floating in the river is incredible to see. Passed three large lodges on the starboard side near which great number of salmon was drying on scaffolds. One of those mat lodges I entered, found it crowded with men, women, and children. I was furnished with a mat to sit on, and one man set about preparing me something to eat.'

Pause.

'The people appear to live in a state of comparative happiness.'

Pause.

JAKE *opens his eyes, looks out to the river.*

(*Distant.*) That's my favorite I guess.

CHRIS *watches him.*

Scene Seven

The parking lot. TRISHA *waits for* CHRIS, *holding two gas-station coffees, smoking a cigarette.*

JAKE *enters. He looks at* TRISHA. TRISHA *nods at him, smiles slightly, then looks away.*

JAKE *is about to walk past her, but then makes a decision and goes to her.*

JAKE. Hey.

> *Pause.*

> TRISHA *turns to him.*

TRISHA (*confused*). Hi?

JAKE. I'm, uh. I work with Chris?

TRISHA. Yeah?

JAKE. I'm a – friend of Chris?

> *Pause.*

TRISHA. Oh.

JAKE. I mean I haven't been working here for very long but we've been – we hang out and – Anyway, hi.

> *Pause.*

> We just got off our shift, he should be out in a minute or so, he's just finishing up with some display stuff.

> *Pause.*

TRISHA. How did you know that I was / his – ?

JAKE. I saw you two talking in the parking lot the other night.

> *Pause.*

> I don't know him very well yet but I know that he's not like, *forthcoming* or whatever about what he's feeling but I know

he cares about you and I – wanted you to know that. That's all.

Pause.

TRISHA *stubs out her cigarette, puts it back in the pack.*

TRISHA. So he's told you all about me then.

JAKE. I mean, sort of –

TRISHA. Crazy drug addict, all that / stuff?

JAKE. *No*, he… He really hasn't, I'm just – I'm just trying to say that he doesn't want to give up on you.

Pause.

TRISHA. He told you that?

JAKE. Yeah. He has.

TRISHA *wanders aimlessly.*

TRISHA. Yeah, well, he's got good reason to give up on me, I guess.

Pause.

I never gave up on him, though. And I could have, believe me. I had him when I was sixteen years old, I could've just sent him to live with his grandparents but I didn't, I refused to give up on him. I have given my *life* to that kid. When his dad left for good, I told him if he ever came back I'd take him down with our shotgun. He knew I meant it, too. One thing you *do not do* is threaten my child. You can do whatever you want to me, I can take whatever, but *not* my kid.

Short pause.

And look I may not be perfect, but neither is he.

JAKE. I mean I don't / really –

TRISHA. I don't know what he's told you about me, but that kid needs me just as much as I need him. Couple years ago he blew outta town, tried to move away, ended up calling me from a Super 8 down in Pocatello, totally freaked out. Drove *ten hours* to go and get him. So don't go thinking that he's some poor *victim* or / whatever –

JAKE. I don't think – Look, sorry, I shouldn't have said anything, I'll just –

JAKE starts to exit, heading toward the Costco. TRISHA takes a step toward him.

TRISHA. *Wait, I'm –*

JAKE stops.

I'm sorry, I shouldn't –

Pause.

He's my favorite guy in the world, but he's not as tough as he looks, you know? So do me a favor, just – make sure he's okay? Keep an eye out for him?

Pause.

JAKE. Yeah, I'll – I will.

Silence. TRISHA takes breath, regards JAKE.

TRISHA. So you two are – ?

Pause.

Shit I'm just not used to this yet.

Pause.

JAKE (*realizing*). Oh, I – I mean we're / not –

TRISHA. He staying with you?

JAKE. *No*, really we're not –

TRISHA. He find a decent place to stay?

JAKE. I mean, I think it's – fine. I think he's fine.

TRISHA. The place is okay, landlord okay?

JAKE. I mean I think it's fine, I don't think he's looking for something very permanent. If grad school works out, I mean.

TRISHA. What?

JAKE. I mean if he ends up going to Iowa, he's not –

TRISHA looks at him. JAKE *realizes, stops himself.*

TRISHA. He's applying to school? In Iowa?

JAKE *looks away.*

JAKE. I don't – *Shit.*

Awkward silence. JAKE *looks to the Costco.*

JAKE. Look, I – Chris'll be here soon, I'm gonna / head home –

TRISHA. I gotta say I'm sorta surprised though.

TRISHA *indicates* JAKE.

JAKE. What?

TRISHA. I just didn't think he'd end up with someone so scrawny.

Pause.

No offense.

Pause.

JAKE. 'Scrawny'?

TRISHA. No offense.

JAKE. When you say something that's completely offensive, saying 'no offense' afterward doesn't make it any less completely / offensive.

TRISHA. Look whatever, he can be into whatever he / wants –

JAKE. Maybe *he's* the lucky one, did you ever think of that?

TRISHA. I'm sure / he is.

JAKE. My IQ is like almost one-forty.

TRISHA. Is it that high?

JAKE. *Yeah it's that high.* I took a test online.

TRISHA. Alright then.

JAKE. And I'm a descendant of *William Clark.*

TRISHA. No shit?

JAKE. *Yeah. So.*

> *Pause.*

> I'm also *funny* and *charming* and *urbane* and –

> CHRIS *enters.*

CHRIS. What the fuck?

JAKE. I was / just –

CHRIS (*to* JAKE). What are you doing?

JAKE. I'm sorry, I'll / just [go] –

TRISHA. I met your [boyfriend] – I didn't think you were, whatever, *seeing* anyone.

CHRIS. *What?*

JAKE. / Oh my God –

TRISHA. I mean it's fine, he's cute. You can put 'im in your pocket.

JAKE (*to* TRISHA). Okay you need to stop because I am *not* that small –

CHRIS. JAKE.

> JAKE *stops, looks at him.*

JAKE. Look I didn't say anything, she just / assumed –

CHRIS. *I'll see you tomorrow, Jake.*

> CHRIS *doesn't look at him.* JAKE *exits. Silence.*

TRISHA. I'm sorry.

CHRIS. Mom.

Pause.

TRISHA. He seems – nice.

Pause.

TRISHA *smiles at him.* CHRIS *smiles despite himself.*

CHRIS. Mom.

TRISHA. I like him! He's a little spitfire, I like him.

CHRIS. Oh my God, mom, can we please / not – ?

TRISHA. I just wanna know who you're – you know! I'm your mom, I wanna make sure you're not seeing some weirdo, or –

CHRIS. Well maybe it's none of your business, and I know it makes you uncomfortable anyway, so maybe just –

TRISHA. Look, I think I'm being pretty good right now, I think I'm being pretty accepting. I know being gay in this town is hard, but it's not easy for me either. People think I did something wrong, like I was a bad mom, or – This bitch Tanya I work with at Denny's? She actually said she was *praying* for you, you believe that? I told her what she could do with her damn –

Pause.

Anyway it's not easy for me either. And I'm trying, is all.

Silence. CHRIS *softens.*

CHRIS. You work yesterday?

TRISHA. Noon to eight.

CHRIS. Everything's – okay?

TRISHA. I mean Trevor's still a dick, I still say he's skimming from the tip pool, but –

Pause.

Yeah, it's fine. Been sleeping like a rock.

CHRIS. That's good.

Pause.

Have you had – cravings or whatever?

TRISHA. Not one. I don't miss it at all.

Pause.

CHRIS. Have you looked into any of the NA programs that I showed you?

TRISHA. Chris, you know that isn't / for me –

CHRIS. If you're gonna do this then you need some support –

TRISHA. Well that's why I'm here, Chris.

CHRIS. Mom this can't all be about *me* –

TRISHA. I know that, I'm just saying –

CHRIS *turns to leave.*

CHRIS. Okay, I can't have this conversation again, I'm going / home –

TRISHA. When were you gonna tell me about Iowa?

Pause. CHRIS *turns to her.*

CHRIS. He told you.

Pause.

TRISHA. Were you just gonna blow outta town without even saying goodbye, that was your plan?

CHRIS. Mom, it wasn't – I just *applied*, I – *Goddammit.*

Pause.

TRISHA. You know what, Chris? You don't need grad school. If you wanna get outta here, let's just *go*, leave town. You and me.

Pause.

CHRIS *looks at her.*

CHRIS. You wanna just – leave?

TRISHA. Why not? Nothing keeping us here.

CHRIS. I have a job here –

TRISHA. You can get a job anywhere, so could I. Plenty of Costcos and Denny's out there. And nothing good ever came out of this town, especially for us. I've got some money saved up from the past couple months. Not a lot, but enough to get us settled.

CHRIS. Where would we go?

TRISHA. I don't know, does it even matter? I say we pack everything up, pick a direction, and just *go*. We're survivors, Chris, you know that – but we need to stick together.

I know you wanna get outta here, but you can't do that alone, you know that.

Pause.

Listen, if we find someplace to go, I'll – I'll get into one of those NA programs you keep telling me about.

CHRIS. Really?

TRISHA. Yeah, why not? Couldn't hurt.

CHRIS. Seriously, if I go with you, you'll get help for this, / you'll – ?

TRISHA. Hand to God, Chris.

Pause.

You don't have to decide right now, I know you've got your – friend here. But just think about it?

Pause.

CHRIS. I'll think about it.

TRISHA. Okay.

TRISHA *smiles at him. She outstretches her arms for a hug, as before.*

CHRIS *looks at her for a moment, then goes to her, hugging her.*

I love you.

CHRIS. I love you too, Mom.

TRISHA. I miss you so much.

CHRIS. I miss you too.

Pause.

I do.

Pause.

They hold one another.

Scene Eight

Electronics: Flat-screen HD Televisions.

The next day. JAKE *is unpacking a box filled with various television accessories: universal remote controls, cords, etc.* CHRIS *enters with a palette on top of which are several 80-inch flat-screen HD televisions, each in massive boxes.*

JAKE *looks at him,* CHRIS *doesn't look back.*

Pause.

JAKE. Look, I'm sorry, I texted you over and over but / you –

CHRIS (*not looking at him*). It's fine.

Pause.

JAKE. Are you really gonna ignore me the entire shift?

CHRIS (*re. the televisions*). Can you lift these?

Pause.

JAKE (*slightly annoyed*). *Yes*, I can lift / them –

CHRIS. Don't get pissy, I just meant with the –

JAKE. *I'm fine.*

CHRIS. Okay, good then.

> CHRIS *moves to one side of one of the televisions, he motions for* JAKE *to move to the other side.*

> *They lift the box, moving it to the shelf.*

JAKE. Look I didn't tell her that we were together, she / just assumed –

CHRIS. Okay, I'd *really* prefer that we didn't talk about this / right now –

JAKE. And I'm sorry about the Iowa thing, I had no idea she didn't know. Seriously, you told me like the first day I met you, I didn't think it was some big –

> *Pause.*

> I just wanted to tell her that you still cared about her, that's all I was trying to do. I was just trying to help.

> *They move the television to the shelf.* CHRIS *stands on the palette, pushing the box to the back to make room for more.*

CHRIS. Look can we just work, okay? How about we just work.

JAKE. Okay.

> *They go to another television, lifting it.*

CHRIS (*quiet*). She knows that I [care about her] –

JAKE. What?

CHRIS. I said *she knows that I care about her.* You just have no idea what you're – You don't know what it's like.

> *They put the television on the shelf.* CHRIS *shoves it to the back.*

JAKE. Look, I can imagine this must be hard.

CHRIS stops working, looks at JAKE.

CHRIS. I worked all through high school, full-time during the summer and after school during the year, to save up for college. Second half of my senior year, she got a hold of my account and blew through all of it in three months. When I was a junior in college, I almost flunked out of a Comp Lit class because she sold my laptop the day before my final paper was due.

Pause.

When I was fourteen, she kicked me out of the house for six days when I flushed her stash. I was so embarrassed I didn't tell anyone, so I slept in the parking lot behind the mall.

Pause.

They look at one another.

After a moment, CHRIS *looks back at the boxes, about to pick up another one. Before he can bend down to get it,* JAKE *goes to him, his arms outstretched.*

Jake, no no no no –

JAKE *wraps his arms around* CHRIS, *embracing him.*

It's awkward at first, CHRIS *is tense and looking around to make sure no one is watching. But after a moment* CHRIS *relaxes into it, accepts it.*

They hug for a moment longer, then JAKE *releases him.* CHRIS *looks away, goes back to the boxes.*

JAKE. Has she ever like gotten *help*, or – ?

CHRIS. She doesn't think she needs help.

Pause. JAKE *goes to the box, lifts the other side. They put it on the shelf.* CHRIS *softens a little.*

I mean it's – It's been better lately, she's clean now.

JAKE. That's good.

Pause.

Has she – ? I mean has she been clean before?

CHRIS. A few times. I told her if she used again then she was out of my life for good.

JAKE. Did you mean it?

Pause.

CHRIS. Probably not. I've said it before.

Pause.

CHRIS *bends down to get another box.* JAKE *grabs the other end, they put it on the shelf.*

She told me yesterday she wants us to move away.

Pause.

JAKE. What do you mean?

CHRIS. Like she wants me to leave town with her, move somewhere else. Make a fresh start.

Pause.

JAKE. You're going to move with her?

CHRIS. I don't know. She said if I went with her she'd go into a program. Maybe she'll actually do it this time, I don't know. It'd probably be good for her to get out of town.

Pause.

JAKE. What about grad school?

CHRIS. Whatever, I can apply some other year.

CHRIS *bends down to get a box, waits for* JAKE *to lift the other end.* JAKE *doesn't move, he looks at* CHRIS.

What?

JAKE. Chris, you can't – You're really gonna do that?

CHRIS. Why not? Nothing's keeping me here.

JAKE. You have a life here.

CHRIS. Not much of one. Plus she needs someone to take care of her, no one else is gonna do it. Are you gonna [lift this with me] – ?

Pause.

JAKE. You realize that you're just her enabler, right?

CHRIS *stands up, looking at* JAKE.

CHRIS. Excuse me?

JAKE. You're just – I mean you tell her that if she uses again then you're gonna leave her for good, but then she uses again and you just forgive her, it's just – You're just allowing her to keep doing this.

Pause.

CHRIS *bends down, grabbing the box.*

CHRIS. Lift it.

JAKE. Chris.

CHRIS. You gonna do your job or not?

JAKE. Look I'm not trying to be a jerk, but if you're gonna tell me how terrible your life is, then I'm going to like try to offer you *solutions* –

CHRIS *stands up, looking at him.*

CHRIS. Okay, you're starting to piss me off.

JAKE. I'm just saying, if you're gonna tell her that she's gonna be out of your life then you should *mean* it, and not – Now she wants you to move away with her, so you can just like *attend* to her addiction in some other town –

CHRIS. Stop acting like you give a fuck about my mom. You're just mad because you think I'm your boyfriend and you don't want me to leave.

Pause.

JAKE. That is / *not true* –

CHRIS. But actually, Jake, I'm *not* your boyfriend, and I won't ever be, so / maybe –

JAKE. I do *not* think that you're my / boyfriend –

CHRIS. Well you told my mom that you were.

JAKE. *I did not tell her that she just / assumed –*

CHRIS. And by the way, I think the whole reason you came here is sort of pathetic.

Silence. CHRIS *stares at him.*

JAKE. What?

CHRIS. I mean so you're like *barely* related to William Clark, who fucking cares? Clark was just some asshole imperialist who wrote some journals and drew some stupid maps, walked across the country just so we could have more shitty fucking towns like this one.

JAKE. Chris, / stop it –

CHRIS. And you come out here, and you can't even fucking *drive* all the way to the ocean without breaking down and threatening to kill yourself to some *stranger*, it's so fucking [pathetic] –

Pause.

I don't even know why you're still here. Are you just sticking around so you can mess with my personal life?

Pause.

Why the fuck are you still here, Jake?

JAKE. Chris, please –

CHRIS. You know what? I don't even care. I don't even know you, I don't care. We're co-workers and that's it, I don't know why I even – Lift the other side.

Pause. CHRIS *goes for another box.*

JAKE. Chris…

CHRIS *goes to* JAKE, *looking at him.*

CHRIS. I don't care. I don't care about you.

Pause.

Lift the fucking box.

CHRIS *goes back to the box. He looks at* JAKE, *waiting for him to lift.*

JAKE, *upset and not knowing what to do, goes to the other side of the box.*

JAKE. Chris, *please.*

CHRIS *doesn't respond to him. They lift the box.*

Just as the box is almost on the shelf, JAKE *suddenly drops his end. The box crashes to the floor, a large shattering sound is heard.*

CHRIS *looks at the box, horrified. He looks at* JAKE. JAKE *stares back at him.*

Oops.

They stare at one another.

Scene Nine

The parking lot, later. JAKE *holds his cellphone. He looks at it for a moment, then makes a call.*

JAKE. Hi, Dad, I'm – Did I wake you up? I'm sorry, it's –

Pause.

Yeah, I'm fine, I – Actually, no, I'm not fine. No, it's not that, I'm taking my meds, I'm safe. And I'm – I'm sorry for leaving like that, I know that wasn't fair of me, I know it was stupid, but I guess I –

Pause.

JAKE *looks out toward the river.*

Dad, I'm – in Washington.

Pause.

No, the state. Eastern Washington, near the Idaho border.

Pause.

Yeah, it's – It's near the trail. I'm actually looking over it right now, it's – kinda beautiful. I mean it's – you know – it's just a little town, I'm standing in a parking lot, but. I don't know, I still think it's sort of beautiful, there's something –

Pause.

JAKE *looks away from the river, staring at the ground.*

I sound – so dumb. I hear that now.

Pause.

I guess – I've been trying to be a different person. The kind of person I've always wanted to be. But I'm kidding myself, I'm not that guy. I'm just a stranger here. And – I need to grow up.

Pause.

I know I can just come home. I know.

JAKE *continues to stare at the asphalt.*

Scene Ten

The parking lot, shortly later, nearing dawn. JAKE stands with his backpack, waiting anxiously. After a moment CHRIS enters. He stops, looks at JAKE.

JAKE. Look I told Janet it was my fault, I told her I wasn't upfront about having Huntington's, and – Look I took the blame, she let me go and we're –

I got fired.

Pause.

CHRIS. We destroyed a five-thousand-dollar television, Jake. We *both* got fired.

JAKE. But that's not – ! I told her it was my fault!

CHRIS. Well since I knew you were sick and I didn't say anything, Janet says that I'm still partially to / blame –

JAKE. You told her that?

CHRIS. I said that I had been covering for you and / that you –

JAKE. Chris, why did you tell her that? You didn't / need to –

CHRIS. Well I didn't think I was gonna be fucking *questioned* today, Jake, I didn't fucking *prepare* my *story* –

JAKE. I'm sorry, I – I'm just sorry.

Pause.

Look, I'm gonna go talk to Janet –

JAKE *starts for the Costco,* CHRIS *blocks him.*

CHRIS. It's done. I'm fired.

Pause.

You just got me fired.

Silence. CHRIS *stares at him,* JAKE *is at a loss.*

You did that on purpose.

Silence. They stare at one another.

JAKE. I was mad.

CHRIS. You fucking / asshole.

JAKE. Look you were being really hurtful, and I didn't know / what to do –

CHRIS. Do you even *know* how much five thousand dollars is?

Pause.

JAKE. What?

CHRIS. That TV you just broke cost five thousand dollars, and what really pisses me off is I don't think you know how much that is. I think – if you needed five thousand dollars? I think you could call up Mommy or Daddy and they would send you five thousand dollars. I think for you five thousand dollars is pretty much meaningless.

JAKE. I know / how much –

CHRIS. Do you know what five thousand dollars is to *me*? Five thousand dollars is what I can put toward my college loans after *eighteen months* of working *full-time*. That's what five thousand dollars means to me. And in your fucking childlike *tantrum*, you *threw it away*.

JAKE sits down on the pavement, his head in his hands.

JAKE. I'm sorry.

CHRIS. Are you?

JAKE. I'm fucked up.

CHRIS (*exasperated*). *Jesus* –

JAKE. I'm really fucked up, Chris, I know I am.

Silence. CHRIS paces.

CHRIS. What are you doing here, Jake? Why did you come here, why did you start working here?

JAKE. I just –

Pause.

I just wanted do the Lewis and Clark trail, to follow it to the ocean – just do this one *last thing* before the Huntington's got really bad. I didn't even tell my mom or my dad what I was doing, I just left, got in my car, but by the time I got out here, I –

Pause.

I couldn't make it.

CHRIS. Why?

JAKE. I almost drove off the road.

Pause.

When I was coming down the grade into town, I almost… I lost control of my leg and I couldn't hit the brake, I – I went up one of those runaway truck ramps, if it had lasted a second longer I probably would have –

Pause.

I barely got into town, pulled into the first hotel I saw. And I realized that the Costco was right across the street, and I thought I could just – work there for a while, do something *real*, wait for the chorea to get better –

Pause.

JAKE *looks at* CHRIS.

I drove out here in *four days*. That's how long it took me. In my nice car with my air-conditioning, stopping for bathroom breaks and Red Bulls and – I realized I've never really had to do anything difficult in my entire life. The one thing I set out to do, to come out here, see the ocean? All I had to do was sit behind a wheel for a few days. And I couldn't even do that. I couldn't even fucking make it.

Pause.

The chorea is getting worse. Yesterday I tried to drive across the bridge, just to get to the spot where Lewis and Clark were camping… I was too scared to leave the parking lot. I feel like I'm fucking *trapped* here.

Pause.

CHRIS *paces.*

CHRIS. This is – This is *really shitty* of you, you know? I mean you got me *fired* tonight and now it's like I'm not even allowed to get mad at you because you're –

Pause.

Fuck.

JAKE. I'm sorry –

CHRIS. Jake, did you – ? You really thought coming out west was a *solution*, you really thought that it would – ? I don't know what kind of magical pioneer land you expected, but this is just some stupid town, it's just –

Pause.

Look you need to understand something. *I can't help you.* Okay? Ever since you came here I feel like you're like asking me for some solution to your problems, but *I don't have it.* My life is pretty shitty right now too, if I knew how to make it better don't you think I would have done it?

JAKE. I'm sorry. I don't deserve your help. I'm sorry.

Pause.

CHRIS. Look, just – Have you talked to your mom or dad?

Pause.

JAKE. I've talked to my dad a few times.

CHRIS. Well just *tell* him, tell him where you are, tell him to buy you a plane ticket or whatever, and *go home*. Okay?

JAKE looks up. He stands up, looking at the river.

JAKE. Yeah I –

Pause.

I guess that's what's gonna happen.

Pause.

CHRIS watches him. TRISHA enters.

CHRIS. Mom, what're you – ?

TRISHA. You got off early! Thought I'd be waiting around for an hour.

Pause.

You okay?

Pause.

CHRIS. We got fired.

Pause.

TRISHA. *Both* of you?

CHRIS. We broke a TV. A very big, very expensive / TV.

JAKE. *I* broke it, it was my [fault] –

Pause.

It was my fault.

Pause.

TRISHA. You know what? This is a good thing, this is perfect timing.

CHRIS *looks at* TRISHA.

CHRIS. What – ?

TRISHA. You remember Melanie?

CHRIS. Melanie?

TRISHA. Yeah, three – four years ago, she stayed with us for a while?

CHRIS. Wait, the – She was married to the biker guy, the / one who – ?

TRISHA. Divorced him three months ago. Best thing that's ever happened to her, really turned her life / around –

CHRIS. Mom, you told me you / wouldn't hang out with –

TRISHA. Outta nowhere yesterday she sends me a text, says she's in town, so I got together with her after work. She's out in Missoula now, she's living in this house with a couple other gals, you might remember one of them. Point is, I was talkin' to her about Missoula – you remember, we went there once when you were a kid, you remember?

CHRIS. No, I don't –

TRISHA. You were little, but I bet you'd remember if you saw
    it, it's so beautiful, and the people are just so nice, and *that's*
    where we can go! We could find work there just as easy as
    we could around here. I'm ready to up and leave, seriously.
    Already told Gary that I'm not gonna be in the apartment
    next month. Told him he can keep the security deposit,
    I don't care, use the money to pay someone to haul all the
    furniture out of there to the dump –

JAKE (*moving to exit*). I can let you guys [talk] –

TRISHA (*to* JAKE). You wanna come with us?

    JAKE *stops.*

JAKE. What?

TRISHA. Fuck it, why not? You got fired too, yeah? I mean
    I don't know how much room Melanie's got in the house, but
    I bet you could find work out there just as easy as you could
    here.

    JAKE *looks at* CHRIS. CHRIS *stares at* TRISHA.

JAKE. I – I mean I / don't –

CHRIS. Mom.

TRISHA. She's there in this house with a couple other gals.
    I know you've met one of them a while back, her name's
    Lydia, she has this big red hair, you'll remember her. And the
    mountains are so pretty, these big mountains / and the –

CHRIS. You're high.

    Silence.

TRISHA. What?

CHRIS. You used.

    Pause.

    Mom, are you high right now?

TRISHA. No!

CHRIS. *Are you high right now?*

TRISHA. Chris I am *not* / high –

CHRIS. Tell me.

   Pause.

TRISHA. Chris –

CHRIS. *Tell me right now.*

   Pause.

TRISHA. Look I'm coming down off it already, Melanie and
   I just did a little bump, it's no big deal.

   CHRIS' *head falls into his chest.*

   Now okay don't – Now don't make this into some big *thing*,
   this isn't like before. Melanie just had this little bit left. She's
   going cold turkey after this, and we just – Okay it was dumb
   of me, but it's not like before, this was just us having some
   fun.

   CHRIS *goes to the ground, sitting on the asphalt, his head
   buried in his hands.*

CHRIS. *Why?*

TRISHA. Chris, I'm sorry, I know I screwed up – but seriously
   it was just this little bit and I'm already comin' down off it,
   so just calm down. No big deal.

   TRISHA *gets down on the ground, putting her arms around
   him.*

CHRIS. Mom.

TRISHA. Okay, now *stop it*, you don't need to – I'm not going
   back to my old habits, this was just one little –

   (*To* JAKE.) Do I look like a junkie to you?

   JAKE *is frozen, unsure of what to do.*

JAKE. I – I mean I / don't –

TRISHA. C'mon, do I look like some addict / who –

CHRIS. *Please. Stop.*

> TRISHA *hugs* CHRIS *tighter.*

TRISHA. Okay, let's just focus on the good stuff, okay? Let's focus on getting ourselves outta Clarkston.

> *Pause.*

> Listen why don't we run by your place, we can grab whatever you wanna take?

> *Silence.*

> CHRIS *finally looks up. He looks at* TRISHA. *TRISHA smiles at him. He looks at* JAKE, *then back at* TRISHA.

> C'mon. Let's go get your stuff –

CHRIS. I can't see you again?

> *Pause.*

> TRISHA *looks at him.*

TRISHA. What?

CHRIS. I can't see you again.

> *Pause.*

> I can't see you again.

> *Pause.*

> TRISHA *stands up.*

> CHRIS *looks up at her.*

> I told you if you used again then you were out of my life –

TRISHA. What're you / saying?

CHRIS. I can't do this anymore.

> *Pause.*

> I'm sorry. I can't do this anymore.

> TRISHA *stares at him, shocked.*

TRISHA. Look, I get it, okay?! I screwed up! I shouldn't have done that, I get it!

CHRIS *looks away from her, staring at the ground.*

Pause.

Chris, I'm going to Missoula right now, with or without you. You don't have a job here, you don't have anything, nothing's keeping you here. We're a team, we've been through worse than this. Let's just *go.*

Pause.

Chris. Let's go.

CHRIS *doesn't move, he continues to stare at the ground.* JAKE *turns away, uncomfortable but feeling compelled to stay with* CHRIS.

TRISHA *looks at him. The reality of the situation slowly begins to dawn on her.*

Silence.

So what, you're *giving up* on me? Is that what you're doing?

Pause.

You know there were a lot of times I could of given up on you, you realize that? You think dad left because I was getting *high*? He left two weeks after he found out you were gay. We've all got our demons, Chris, I accepted yours.

CHRIS *lies down on the asphalt, curling up into the fetal position, facing upstage.* TRISHA *bears down on him, shouting.*

FINE, I DON'T NEED YOU. STAY HERE WITH YOUR FUCKIN' *BOYFRIEND*, YOUR –

TRISHA *stops herself, taking a few breaths. She looks at* JAKE, *who continues to look away.*

Silence. She turns to leave.

I'm done, to hell with this.

TRISHA *stops, turns back to* CHRIS, *her anger dissolved into a deep sadness.*

Silence.

(*Pleading.*) *Chris, please.*

Pause.

Christopher.

Pause.

Christopher.

Pause.

Chris.

CHRIS *doesn't move.* TRISHA *looks at him for a moment longer, then finally turns and exits. After a moment we hear the sound of a car door shutting, an engine starting, a car driving off.*

Silence.

JAKE *looks at* CHRIS, *who remains curled up, facing upstage.* JAKE *cautiously approaches him.*

Finally:

JAKE. Chris.

Pause.

She's gone, Chris.

CHRIS *doesn't move.* JAKE *looks down on him, not knowing what to say.*

I don't – I don't want to leave you.

Pause.

Is it okay if I don't leave you?

Pause.

CHRIS *doesn't respond.* JAKE *paces.*

You know, maybe this is all like – I mean maybe this is a good thing. For both of you. I mean in a few months you might be getting your MFA out in Iowa, spending your days writing / stories and –

CHRIS. I didn't get in.

Pause.

JAKE. What?

CHRIS. I got a rejection letter. Two days ago.

Pause.

JAKE. Oh.

Pause.

Well look I mean there's like waitlists, and –

CHRIS. I didn't get waitlisted. I got rejected. It was a form letter.

Pause.

It came early. Which means I got rejected in the first round.

Pause. JAKE *cautiously sits down on the ground next to* CHRIS.

JAKE *reaches over to put a hand on* CHRIS' *shoulder, but stops himself. He looks out to the river, trying to think of what to say.*

JAKE. I'll just sit with you. I'll sit with you for a while. Is that okay?

Pause.

CHRIS *doesn't respond.* JAKE *continues to watch the river.*

Okay.

Pause.

Can I read another one of your stories? I could read it out loud?

CHRIS. *No.*

JAKE. Okay, sorry, I –

Silence.

Finally, JAKE *opens his backpack, taking out the book from before.*

I can read you some more from the journals? You wanna hear some more?

Pause.

CHRIS *doesn't respond.*

JAKE *opens up the book, flips a few pages.*

August 24th, 1804.

(*Reading.*) 'One evidence which the Indians give for believing this place to be the residence of some unusual spirits is that they frequently discover a large assemblage of birds around this mound – is in my opinion a sufficient proof to produce in the savage mind a confident belief of – '

(*Stops, flips pages.*) Okay maybe something less racist maybe. Okay – May 15th, 1805.

(*Reading.*) 'We saw buffalo on the banks dead, others floating down dead, and others mired every day, those buffalo either drown in swimming the river or – '

(*Stops reading.*) Okay let's just – Let's just get them to the ocean, maybe that'll be more optimistic.

JAKE *flips a few pages, landing on something.*

Okay here.

(*Reading.*) 'Great joy in camp. We are now in view of the ocean, this great Pacific Ocean which we have been so long anxious to see. And the roaring or noise made by the waves breaking on the rocky shores, as I suppose, may be heard distinctly. We made thirty-four miles today as computed.'

Pause.

'Notwithstanding the disagreeable time of the party for several days past, they are all cheerful and full of anxiety to see further into the ocean. The water is too salt to drink, we use rainwater.'

CHRIS *lifts himself up slightly off the ground, pulling himself toward* JAKE, *still facing upstage. He rests his head in* JAKE's *lap.* JAKE *watches him for a moment, then goes back to reading.*

(*Reading.*) 'November 19th, 1805. I arose early this morning from under a wet blanket caused by a shower of rain which fell in the latter part of the last night, and sent two men on ahead with directions to proceed on near the sea coast and kill something for breakfast. After drying our blankets a little I set out with a view to proceed near the coast. The bay was at no great distance across. I overtook the hunters at about three miles, they had killed a small deer on which we had breakfast.'

Pause. JAKE *raises his hand, considers placing it on the side of* CHRIS' *head. He stops, puts his hand down.*

(*Reading.*) 'After taking a sumptuous breakfast of venison – '

CHRIS. 'Sumptuous'? It says that?

Pause.

JAKE. Yeah.

CHRIS. That's funny.

JAKE. Yeah.

JAKE *gently puts his hand on* CHRIS' *head as he reads.*

(*Reading*). 'After taking a sumptuous breakfast of venison which was roasted on sticks exposed to the fire, I proceeded on through rugged country of high hills and steep hollers on a course from the cape, north twenty degrees west, five miles on a direct line to the commencement of a sandy coast which extended north ten degrees west from the top of the hill above the sand shore to a point of high land distant near twenty miles. This point I have taken the liberty of calling after my particular friend Lewis.'

CHRIS *rolls over, facing downstage, his head still in* JAKE*'s lap. He watches the river.*

(*Reading.*) 'I proceeded on the sandy coast four miles, and marked my name on a small pine, the day of the month and year, et cetera, and returned to the foot of this hill, from which place I intended to strike across the bay. I saw a sturgeon which had been thrown on shore and left by the tide ten feet in length, and several joints of the back bone of a whale which must have been foundered on – '

CHRIS. They camped right over there?

JAKE *looks up, across the river, to where* CHRIS *is looking.*

Pause.

JAKE. Yeah. Right over there.

Silence.

CHRIS. That's neat.

Pause.

They look over the river.

Scene Eleven

Several weeks later.

For the first time, the space feels open, bright, and natural. The sound of the river has been replaced by the sound of ocean waves crashing against a rocky shoreline.

CHRIS *and* JAKE *stand together on the sand, barefoot.*

Silence as they look over the ocean.

JAKE. Is it what you expected?

CHRIS. I guess. I mean I've seen pictures so it's not too surprising. It's nice.

Pause.

JAKE. Thanks for driving me out here.

CHRIS. Sure. I've never seen it either.

Silence. They look for a moment longer, then CHRIS *starts to leave.*

You ready?

JAKE *looks at him.*

JAKE. What, you're *done*?

CHRIS. Yeah?

JAKE. We've been here for like ten minutes.

CHRIS. I mean we've *seen* it, so.

JAKE. It took us *eight hours* to drive here and you wanna leave after ten minutes?!

CHRIS *looks out to the ocean.*

CHRIS. I like it, it's nice! It's just – I mean there it is, I've seen it. It's what I expected it to look like, it's what it looks like in the photographs.

JAKE. Oh my God I don't understand you.

CHRIS. Look I just don't want to be driving in the dark / and we –

JAKE *stands up.*

JAKE. Okay, stop. It's the Fourth of July, it's your day off, relax for Christ's sake. Just – look.

They both look out to the ocean.

CHRIS. Yeah?

JAKE. I mean think what it was like for Lewis and Clark when they got here, and they *hadn't* seen a photograph. It was just all – *new*.

CHRIS. It must have been awesome. But I *have* seen a photograph of it so –

JAKE. Yeah I'm asking you to fucking pretend. Pretend like you're seeing all this for the first time.

They both look out to the ocean.

CHRIS. I mean it's nice.

JAKE sighs, exasperated.

What?!

JAKE. Never mind.

Pause.

Well I think it's – I've never seen it and I think it's pretty amazing. I feel like I'm seeing it for the first time, and it's –

JAKE has a sudden involuntary movement in his leg, he grabs it. CHRIS watches him.

JAKE takes a few deep breaths.

CHRIS. You okay?

JAKE. Yeah, I just –

Pause.

I really hate this.

CHRIS. I know.

Pause.

JAKE punches his leg in frustration, CHRIS goes to him.

Okay, okay –

Silence. JAKE looks out to the ocean. CHRIS watches him.

JAKE. You know what's really weird? I've actually never been able to picture myself getting old.

Pause.

CHRIS. What do you mean?

JAKE. I mean even when I was little, I – I could picture myself being a teenager, I could picture myself being in my twenties, but I – I just could never picture myself actually – I guess somewhere in my brain I've always known I wouldn't live very long.

Pause.

It's like – I should be having some big revelation now, some epiphany about what to do with the years that I have left, but I – I don't.

Pause.

Do you think that makes me a pathetic person?

Pause.

CHRIS *goes to him.*

CHRIS. Don't be so hard on yourself? You're not dying tomorrow. And I'll be around, you know.

JAKE. For a while. Until you get into grad school somewhere, move away, start getting old.

Pause.

I guess I have no idea what's in front of me. That feels new, at least.

Pause.

JAKE *looks out to the ocean for a moment, then takes out his iPhone.*

JAKE. Here, you want your picture with the ocean in the background?

CHRIS. Oh, no.

Pause.

JAKE *looks at him.*

JAKE. You don't / want your – ?

CHRIS. I mean I just don't want it to be a whole *thing*, like you take a photo and post it online and people fucking *comment /* on it and –

JAKE. I won't post it online, oh my God.

CHRIS. I also just – I don't like having my picture taken.

JAKE. Okay we'll take it together.

JAKE stands next to him.

CHRIS. Jake, c'mon –

JAKE. Shut up I hate you.

JAKE fiddles with his iPhone, turning the camera on. He swaps the screen so that the front-facing camera is turned on.

Here, you have longer arms.

He gives the iPhone to CHRIS, who reluctantly takes it. They stand next to one another, facing upstage. CHRIS holds up the iPhone so we see their faces on the screen. He snaps a quick photo.

CHRIS. There.

He gives the iPhone to JAKE.

JAKE (*looking at the photo*). Oof, no. Take it again.

CHRIS. *Jake.*

JAKE. You look like an *ogre* in this photo. You look like you're going to go eat some babies.

CHRIS. Shut up gimme the [phone] –

CHRIS takes the phone again. They pose again for the shot. CHRIS raises the phone.

JAKE. Relax!

JAKE puts an arm around him. CHRIS relaxes, smiles a bit. He takes a photo of the two of them, gives the phone to JAKE. JAKE looks at it.

There. It's nice! See?

JAKE *hands the phone to* CHRIS, *he looks at it. Silence.*

What?

CHRIS *doesn't respond, still looking at the photo.*

You okay?

CHRIS. Yeah, I –

Pause.

CHRIS *looks at the photo. He takes a few steps toward the water.*

I'm just realizing – I think up until this second I never thought I'd see the ocean.

Pause.

I didn't realize that I thought that.

Pause.

JAKE *takes a few steps forward, joining* CHRIS.

They continue to look out to the ocean.

End of play.